LEABHARLANNA FHINE GALL
FINGAL LIBRARIES

Items should be returned on or before the given return date. Items may be renewed in branch libraries, by phone or online. You will need your PIN to renew online. Fines are charged on overdue items. Damage to, or loss of items, will be charged to the borrower.

SPORTING HEROES

NEYMAR

ROY APPS

ILLUSTRATED BY ALESSANDRO VALDRIGHI

EDGE

FRANKLIN WATTS

LONDON·SYDNEY

Franklin Watts
First published in Great Britain in 2017
by The Watts Publishing Group

Text © Roy Apps 2017
Illustrations © Watts Publishing Group 2017
Cover design by Peter Scoulding
Executive Editor: Adrian Cole

*The statistics in this book were correct at the time
of printing, but because of the nature of the sport,
it cannot be guaranteed that they are now accurate.*

HB ISBN 978 1 4451 5314 8
PB ISBN 978 1 4451 5317 9
Library ebook ISBN 978 1 4451 5316 2

1 3 5 7 9 10 8 6 4 2

Printed in China

Franklin Watts
An imprint of
Hachette Children's Group
Part of The Watts Publishing Group
Carmelite House
50 Victoria Embankment
London EC4Y 0DZ

An Hachette UK Company
www.hachette.co.uk

www.franklinwatts.co.uk

I KNOW HE'S ONLY YOUNG. BUT WOULD YOU BE HAPPY FOR ME TO TAKE HIM FOR SOME COACHING SESSIONS?

DAD?

SURE. BUT WE'LL HAVE TO ASK HIS MOTHER FIRST.

CHAPTER TWO
FOOTBALL CRAZY

Neymar lived with his parents and little sister Rafaella in a small house, which his father had built. Neymar's father's career as a professional footballer had been cut short by injury. Now he worked as a mechanic, but sometimes it was difficult to pay the bills.

One evening, after Neymar's mum had allowed him to train with Betinho, Neymar switched on the TV. Nothing happened.

'Mum! The TV's not working!'

'The electricity company has cut us off,' his mum explained. 'We just don't have enough money to pay the bill.'

Every evening, while the electricity was off, Neymar's mother lit candles around the house. In the semi-darkness, Neymar's father told Neymar and Rafaella stories about his days as a pro footballer. It was a magical time.

Neymar started playing for local boys' club Portuguesa Santista. Any spare time was spent kicking a ball about on the beach or in the street. His cousins and other kids from the neighbourhood joined in — sometimes five a side, sometimes fifteen a side! The biggest kids played as strikers, the fastest as wingers and the youngest as goalposts.

NEYMAR! WHAT WILL YOUR FATHER SAY!

BRRRRMMMM

QUICK! HE'S BACK FROM WORK!

'Go to bed!' his mum ordered. 'Pretend you're asleep! Your father won't dare wake you up.'

For two weeks, Neymar went to bed early, pretending to be asleep, just so that his father wouldn't tell him off for ruining his lawn.

When Neymar's father eventually spoke to his son, he wasn't as angry as Neymar thought he would be.

'Don't forget, I was a footballer. I understand how frustrating it is for you, not having a proper pitch to play on, but you're only young. One day, a professional club will take you on, I'm sure of it.'

Neymar continued to practise his ball skills in the garden. This time he used a small, lightweight tennis ball, and kicked it against the fence with his left

foot; then his right foot; then his thigh.

Then he sat down, dejectedly. Would he ever get the chance to play football in a proper team?

CHAPTER THREE

ZITO

When Neymar wasn't outside playing football in the garden, on the beach or in the street, he was inside playing futsal. Betinho saw it as an important part of training.

Spectators rarely watched futsal, but one day Neymar noticed an old guy standing at the side of the hall where they were playing. He looked vaguely familiar.

'It's someone's grandfather — or great-grandfather,' thought Neymar.

At the end of the match, Neymar saw the old man go up to Betinho. The two of them hugged, like they were old friends. Betinho beckoned across the hall to where Neymar's father was standing. Neymar Senior went over and shook the old man's hand. The three men had a brief conversation, then Neymar's father called his son over.

'So, this is your Juninho?' said the old man.

'Juninho,' said Neymar's father. 'Let me introduce you to Zito.'

Neymar couldn't believe what he was hearing. Zito? *The* Zito? Jose Ely de Miranda, or 'Zito', had been part of the Brazilian national side that won the World Cup in 1958 and 1962.

CHAPTER FOUR
SANTOS

For the 11-year-old Neymar, playing and training with Santos was like being in another world. For a start, it was a big club, one of only five never to have been relegated from the Brazilian top-tier of football. Most famously, though, it was the club where footballing legend Pelé had started his career.

As Zito had warned, playing football at Santos was very different to playing for a local boys' sports club team. There was no squad for the under-13s, so Neymar played with the under-15s. The matches were tough, the defenders in the opposition team always bigger and stronger.

'It's good for him,' said Neymar's father.

'Maybe,' replied Zito. 'But he's more likely to develop his skills playing with boys his own age. I've suggested the club should start an under-13 team, and they've agreed.'

A number of the boys who joined the under-13 squad lived near Neymar. Betinho would drop them back home after a hard day's training.

Santos was a club well-known for producing talented young footballers. Scouts from other clubs would often be on the touchline, watching matches. Neymar was already being talked about as a star in the making. It would only be a matter of time before a larger club started showing an interest in him.

Neymar was just 14 years old, when Zito took him and his father aside after training one afternoon. In his hand he held a large brown envelope.

'Another club wants to have a look at you, Juninho,' said Zito.

'A big club?' asked Neymar.

'They don't get much bigger than this,' replied Zito.

He gave the envelope to Neymar.

'In here are two first-class airline tickets to Madrid in Spain. Real Madrid CF want to give you a trial!'

CHAPTER FIVE
REAL MADRID

'Fasten your seatbelts. We are about to begin our descent into Madrid-Barajas Airport.'

Neymar clipped on his seatbelt, then looked out of the window as the aircraft dropped through wispy clouds towards the sprawling city beneath them. He had never flown before; never been out of South America before.

'How are you feeling, Juninho?' his father asked.

'Yeah, excited...' Neymar replied. 'But a bit scared, I guess. Supposing I mess up?'

'You won't mess up, son.'

'Easy to say,' Neymar thought, 'but I've got just over a fortnight to prove myself to the coaches at Real Madrid, one of the biggest football clubs in the world.'

The very next day, Neymar went straight into training. He met the big stars from Real's first team, including David Beckham. In each training match he played, Neymar scored goals. Within just three days, Real had drawn up a contract for Neymar: the whole family would move to Spain with financial support from the club. Neymar's father signed the papers and shook hands with the club's lawyer.

'Is that it?' asked Neymar.

'Not quite,' said his father. 'Your mother has to sign, too.'

Neymar's mother and little sister were still at home in Brazil.

A FEW DAYS LATER, NEYMAR'S FATHER NOTICED THAT HIS SON WAS LACKING PACE. HE SEEMED UNHAPPY...

ARE YOU OK, JUNINHO? YOU'RE NOT GOING DOWN WITH A COLD OR ANYTHING?'

I'M FINE!

I'VE SEEN HAPPIER LOOKING TURKEYS AT CHRISTMAS.

CHAPTER SIX
BARCELONA

If Neymar thought he could simply go back to Santos, and quietly get on with playing for the under-15s, he was mistaken. He made headline news!

Over two years after turning down Real, Neymar was still playing for the Santos youth team. The club's fans wondered what was going on.

'If he's that good, why isn't he in the first team?'

'Perhaps he's not as good as they thought he'd be.'

The fans weren't the only ones who were frustrated.

'When will I get a chance in the first team?' Neymar asked the manager.

'When you're ready,' was always the reply.

Santos were going through a bad patch, and the new manager didn't want to take any chances with a young untried player, not even a talented one like Neymar.

Eventually, though, in 2009, Neymar made his professional debut in the Santos FC first team. It was an away match, but there were a few thousand Santos fans in the stadium.

Neymar came off the bench. He went for goal with his first touch.

'Awwww...'

His rasping shot came off the post!

Two games later, Neymar scored his first professional goal. He was just 17 years old.

The goals continued to come. The following season, Neymar scored five goals as Santos thumped Guaraní 8–1 in a Brazilian Cup match.

At the end of the season, Neymar and his father were called in for a meeting with the Santos club president.

'We've had an offer for you, Juninho,' the president said. 'A very good offer, from Chelsea FC. We wouldn't stand in your way, if you wanted to go.'

It was a tough call. Neymar was 18 now; an adult. He felt he'd be happy leaving home and moving to England, especially if he was playing for a club like Chelsea.

But then he thought again…

'Would I be playing for Chelsea, or would I be loaned out, like a lot of their young players?'

In the end, Neymar decided, once again, to stay at Santos. That season, he helped them win the league title, scoring 20 goals. FC Barcelona contacted the club, but Neymar wasn't going anywhere.

For two years running, in 2011 and 2012, he was voted South American Footballer of the Year. Early in 2013, he got a call from the club president.

'Barca have called again.'

Neymar felt ready. It was finally time for him to spread his wings.

'I'm happy to talk to them,' he said.

CHAPTER SEVEN
AGONY

On the 3rd June 2013, Neymar Junior was presented at the Camp Nou in front of 56,000 cheering Barcelona fans.

Ten weeks later, he scored his first competitive goal for the club. It was a cup match, against Atlético Madrid. The following month, he scored his first La Liga goal as Barcelona beat Real Sociedad 4—1.

By the time the 2014 World Cup kicked off in Brazil, Neymar had been at Barcelona for 11 months. Expectations amongst the home fans were high. Everyone reckoned that Neymar, by now one of Brazil's star players, would play a big part in helping his country win their sixth World Cup.

Brazil's first match was against Croatia. Croatia took an early lead through a Brazilian own goal. The Brazilian fans — and the players — were already getting panicky. Croatia broke again. Putting in a desperate tackle, Neymar appeared to elbow the Croatian midfielder Modrić.

'Off! Off!' bellowed the Croatian fans.

The referee put his hand in his pocket. Luckily for Neymar, it was just a yellow — and not a red — card. Ten minutes later, Neymar equalised for Brazil with a shot from outside the box. In the second half he also scored a penalty, as Brazil ran out 3—1 winners. The home crowd went wild.

'Neymar! Neymar!'

Brazil progressed to the quarter finals where they played Colombia. After just seven minutes, Brazil won a corner.

Neymar swung his corner kick into the far side of the box; one bounce and Brazil's captain Thiago Silva struck the ball into the Colombia goal.

'Goal!!! Y-e-e-s-s-!!!'

It soon started to become a very physical and hard-fought match. With less than ten minutes to go to full-time, and with Brazil winning 2–1, Neymar challenged for the ball. He was kneed in the back by Colombian wing-back, Juan Zúñiga. Neymar crashed to the ground, screaming in agony. The referee waved for the team doctor to come on. The doctor took one look at Neymar and called for a stretcher.

Neymar's World Cup was over.

CHAPTER EIGHT
MSN

At the hospital, a scan revealed that Neymar had fractured a bone in his back.

'You're a very lucky man,' the doctor told him.

'Lucky?' exclaimed Neymar, almost crying.

'Yes, lucky.' The doctor pointed to the scan. 'Just two centimetres closer to the middle of your back and you would not have been able to walk again.'

In the World Cup semi-final, Brazil lost to Germany, 7—1.

Neymar, like every other Brazilian, was heartbroken.

Neymar recovered quickly from his broken back. At the end of September, just three months after being stretchered off the pitch in the World Cup, he scored a hat-trick for Barcelona.

There was a buzz of excitement around the Camp Nou.

'This could be a special year!'

'Neymar has really hit his stride.'

It wasn't just Neymar's sparkling form that was getting fans excited. After a full season in the team, he was beginning to form a real partnership and a real understanding with Barcelona's two other star strikers, Lionel Messi and Luis Suárez.

'Messi! Suárez! Neymar!' cheered the fans.

Soon, they shortened this to M S N.

'M, S, N! M, S, N!'

By the middle of May 2015, Barcelona had won La Liga. By the end of May,

they had won the Copa del Rey, the Spanish Cup. On the 6th June they beat Juventus to win the UEFA Champions League.

Between them, M S N had scored a total of 122 goals; 39 of those — including ten in the Champions League, came from Neymar.

The young boy from Brazil, who had begun playing football on the beaches and back streets of his seaside home, was now truly a sporting legend.

SPORTING 🏆 HEROES

FACT FILE

Full name: Neymar da Silva Santos Júnior

Nickname: Juninho

Date of birth: 5th February 1992

Place of birth: Mogi das Cruzes, Brazil

Height: 1.75m (5ft 7in)

GLOSSARY

fortnight — two weeks

futsal — a version of five-a-side football, usually played indoors, and very popular in Brazil

loaned out — sent to play for another team for a set period of time

Pelé — Brazilian football player, widely thought to be the best in the world

relegated — move down from a higher division to a lower one at the end of a season

scouting — looking for talented football players, usually in youth teams

touchline — line marking the outer edge of a football pitch

CAREER

Key trophies won at Santos:

Campeonato Paulista	2010, 2011, 2012
Copa do Brasil	2010
Copa Libertadores	2011
Recopa Sudamericana	2012

Trophies won at FC Barcelona:

La Liga	2014—15, 2015—16
Copa del Rey	2014—15, 2015—16
Supercopa de España	2013, 2016
UEFA Champions League	2014—15
UEFA Super Cup	2015
FIFA Club World Cup	2015

International Trophies:

South American Youth Championship	2011
Brazilian Golden Ball	2011
FIFA Confederations Cup and Golden Ball award	2013
Olympic Gold	2016

Top Individual Honours:

World Soccer Young Player of the Year	2011
FIFA Puskás Award (Best Goal of the Year)	2011
South American Footballer of the Year	2011, 2012
Bola de Ouro	2012
UEFA Champions League Top Scorer*	2014—15
Samba Gold	2014—15

*Tied with Cristiano Ronaldo and Lionel Messi

It was scary. Lonely. On the streets at night. There were noises everywhere. Cars and taxis hooting, buses revving, people calling out and shouting.

One night, while Fara was curled up under the arches down by the river, an old guy came and sat down beside her... He looked hard at the football boots Fara was clutching.

'Nice boots. Do you play?'

Fara nodded. 'For Chelsea Ladies...'

CONTINUE READING *FARA'S* AMAZING STORY IN...

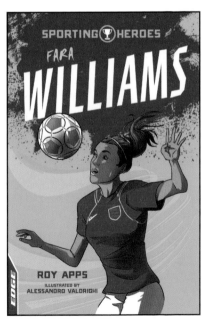

SPORTING HEROES
FARA
WILLIAMS

ROY APPS
ILLUSTRATED BY
ALESSANDRO VALDRIGHI